GW01396202

First Rainforest Book

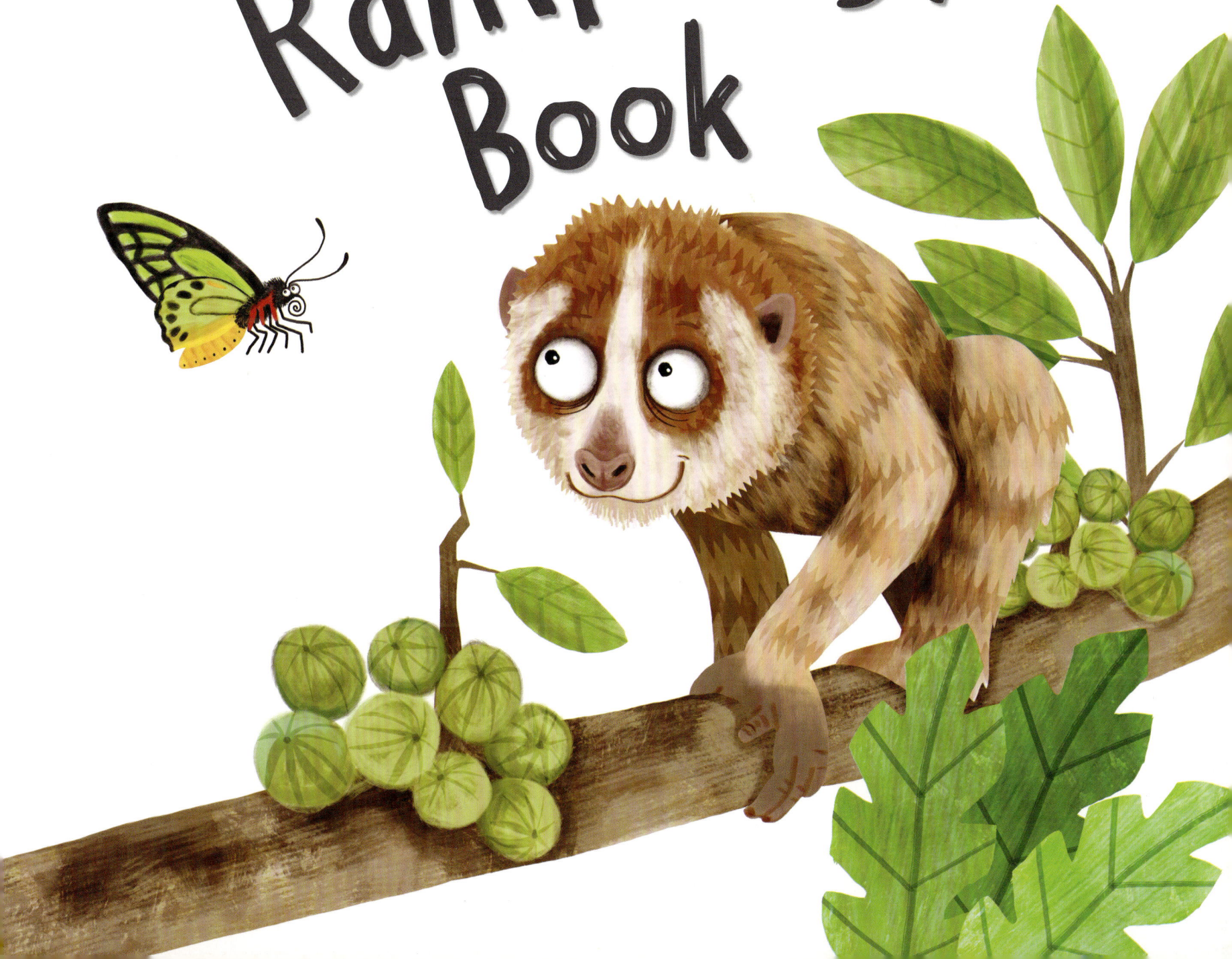

Meet a strange, egg-laying mammal on page 42.

First published in 2022 by Miles Kelly Publishing Ltd
Harding's Barn, Bardfield End Green, Thaxted, Essex, CM6 3PX, UK

Copyright © Miles Kelly Publishing Ltd 2022

2 4 6 8 10 9 7 5 3 1

Publishing Director Belinda Gallagher
Creative Director Jo Cowan
Editorial Director Rosie Neave
Managing Designer Joe Jones
Production Jennifer Brunwin
Image Manager Liberty Newton
Reprographics Stephan Davis
Assets Lorraine King

All rights reserved. No part of this publication may be reproduced, stored in a retrieval system, or transmitted by any means, electronic, mechanical, photocopying, recording, or otherwise, without the prior permission of the copyright holder.

ISBN 978-1-78989-208-6

Printed in China

British Library Cataloguing-in-Publication Data
A catalogue record for this book is available from the British Library

Made with paper from a sustainable forest

www.mileskelly.net

See a chimp teaching her baby to use tools on page 36.

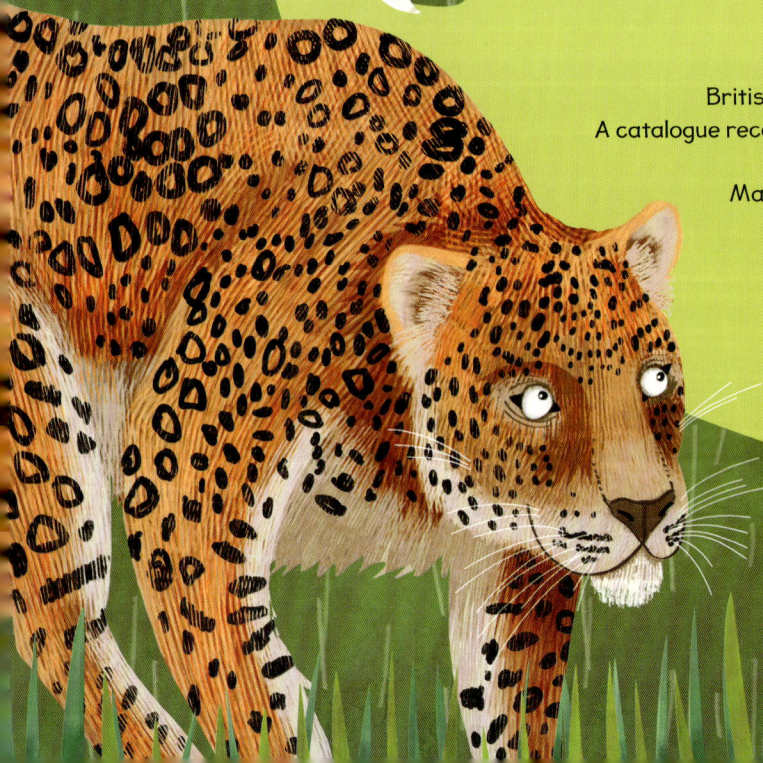

Find out why armadillos have such thick skin on page 23.

First Rainforest Book

Camilla de la Bédoyère

Illustrated by Elissambura

Miles Kelly

Contents

I'm a marsupial, so I carry my baby in a special pouch.

If I was as strong as an ant I could easily lift a baby elephant!

What are you doing to protect rainforests?

It's raining!

It doesn't just rain in a rainforest, it pours! Most rainforests grow in warm places where rain clouds burst open almost every day, drenching everything.

Jungle life

Forests are full of plants that battle to reach the sunlight. Together, they make a perfect home for a huge variety of animals, from busy ants to hungry elephants.

We love a shower!

Some rainforests have more than 10 metres of rain in a year!

At least 2 metres of rain falls every year in a rainforest.

There are tasty flowers, fruits and seeds everywhere! Yum!

I've made my own umbrella!

Jungle home

A rainforest is a type of habitat, or home. There are lots of places to live and plenty of food to eat.

All the animals and plants in a forest need each other to survive. This is called an ecosystem.

I CAN... MEASURE RAINFALL!

Put a container outside, and measure the contents at the same time each day. Keep a rain diary to record how much rain falls in a week.

I like to swim in the rainwater that collects inside this plant.

7

Where in the world?

Great Bear Rainforest

More than a million types of animals live in **forests**.

Temperate rainforests grow in cooler places.

North America

Atlantic Ocean

Africa

Monteverde Cloud Forest

Congo Rainforest

Most rainforests grow in the tropics – near the Equator, between the Tropic of Cancer and the Tropic of Capricorn (yellow). Here, climates are usually hot, sunny and wet.

Amazon Rainforest

The **Amazon Rainforest** is the world's **biggest** tropical forest.

South America

Super seasons
Temperate places have four seasons: spring, summer, autumn and winter. Tropical places only have wet or dry seasons.

Pacific Ocean

KEY
- Tropical rainforest
- Temperate rainforest
- Equator
- (Upper) Tropic of Cancer
- (Lower) Tropic of Capricorn

Arctic Ocean

Europe

There are no tropical rainforests in Europe.

Asia

Nearly **half** of the world's forests grow in **tropical** areas.

I CAN... FIND MY HABITAT

Look at the map to find where you live. Are you in a tropical or temperate part of the world? What words can you use to describe your climate?

The Equator is an invisible line that cuts the planet into two halves.

Borneo Rainforest

The climate is an area's pattern of weather over a long period of time.

Indian Ocean

← **Madagascar Rainforest**

Oceania

Daintree Rainforest

There are about 3,000,000,000,000 trees on Earth – that's 3 trillion!

Southern Ocean

Rainforests in trouble

The world's rainforests are precious homes for animals, plants and people. Sadly, we are in danger of losing many forests and their animals forever.

I'm a Philippine eagle. There may be fewer than 500 of us left.

I CAN... TRY TO USE LESS PAPER

Try to re-use paper at least once before putting it out to be recycled. Old packaging can become wrapping paper, and the backs of letters are great for drawing on.

Spix's macaw

Cut and burn

Half of all forests have disappeared in the last 2000 years, because humans are cutting down trees. This is called deforestation.

10

Rainforests increase the amount of water in the air, which helps to keep the planet cooler.

Dirty air

Pollution in the air is making Earth warmer. This is called global climate change. When rainforest climates change, there is less rain, and the trees die.

Sumatran rhino

If our forest is cut down we'll have nowhere to live.

Many rainforest animals are endangered, which means they may die out forever.

We cut down trees to make space to grow crops (other plants that we use), or to use their wood to make things like paper, or as fuel.

I'm an okapi. Some people hunt rainforest animals, like me, for food.

okapi

Ancient forests

Step into an ancient habitat, where hungry dinosaurs once hunted. Australia's Daintree Forest is 180 million years old, making it one of the oldest rainforests in the world.

canopy

1 Rainforests are divided into levels. The tallest treetops are the **emergent** layer. The **canopy** is a thick layer of branches and leaves.

understorey

2 Smaller trees and shrubs grow in the **understorey**.

Flutter by, butterfly

The wings of a Ulysses butterfly flash with a stunning blue. Can you spot its green caterpillar hiding in the plants of the understorey?

I eat bugs by biting them and sucking their insides out. I also squirt slime!

3 The **forest floor** is at the bottom.

Squirty worms

Velvet worms have up to 43 pairs of feet and have been around for 500 million years! They live on the forest floor.

forest floor

Tree Kangaroo

I can climb trees, even with a wriggly baby in my pouch!

The massive **cassowary** bird can't fly, but it can deliver a deadly kick! It finds food in the understorey and on the forest floor.

My sharp claws grow to 10 centimetres long!

The Kuku Yalanji people have lived in this part of Australia for 50,000 years.

I CAN... NAME FOUR MARSUPIALS

A marsupial mum keeps her joey (baby) in a pouch. The babies are tiny when they are born. Find out the names of four Australian marsupial species.

A wonderful wilderness

The Great Bear Rainforest in Canada is sometimes called the Amazon of the North. It's a temperate rainforest, so it can be hot, warm or even icy-cold. In winter, the mountains have snowy caps.

More than 6 metres of rain falls every year, making this one of the world's wettest forests.

Foggy forest

The tops of tall trees are often hidden here. Warm, wet air is blown in from the ocean and bumps into cool air alongside the mountains. This turns the wet air into fog.

Many birds visit rainforests when they go on long journeys, which are called **migrations**.

I'm one of six million birds that visit the Great Bear Rainforest every year.

Western tanager

Varied thrush

14

GOSHaWK

I'm waiting for the chance to grab any fishy scraps to feed my chicks.

I CAN... MAKE RAIN

Ask an adult to half fill a glass jar with very hot water. Place a plate on top of the jar, wait 30 seconds, then put ice cubes on top of the plate. The cold will turn the warm air into water droplets inside the jar — that's how rain is made!

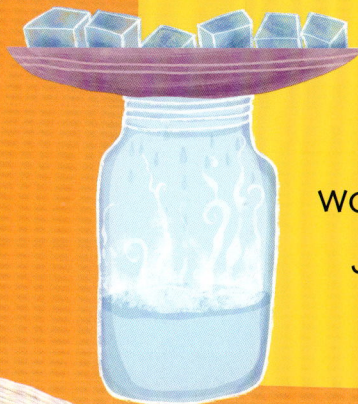

Spirit bears are a creamy-white variant of **black bears**. They are also called **kermode bears**.

We swim up the rivers to find places to lay our eggs — but we have to avoid the bears!

salmon

15

Cloud forest

The trees in a cloud forest are cloaked in a mist that blocks out much of the sunlight. They grow on mountains in tropical places.

Not much sunlight can pass through the clouds, so the air feels COLD and DAMP.

Three-toed sloth

I hang upside down and nibble on leaves. I move so slowly that tiny plants can grow in my fur, giving me a greenish glow!

Moss is a small plant that grows well in dark, damp places

Green and lush

This is the Monteverde Cloud Forest in Costa Rica, Central America. The trees are covered in moss.

Plenty of plants

Orchids (1), bromeliads (2) and ferns (3) grow well in damp, warm air. There are more than 420 species of orchids here and 60 types of avocado tree!

16

My spotty coat helps me to stay hidden in the shadows.

Tapirs

I'm a quetzal – say 'Kay-tal'! It took three years for my beautiful tail feathers to grow this long.

We snuffle in the undergrowth, looking for fruit and leaves to eat.

Agoutis are the only animals that can crack open the nuts of a Brazil nut tree.

Agouti

I CAN... MAKE A QUETZAL COLLAGE

Collect small pieces of colourful waste paper. Draw the outline of a quetzal and use glue to decorate your bird with the pieces of collage paper. Cut out your finished artwork to make a bird hanging.

Stinky grease coats my fur and works like a raincoat to keep my skin dry.

The mighty Congo

Central Africa's Congo Rainforest is huge. It surrounds the Congo River, which is so long that it takes six months to reach the Atlantic Ocean from its source in the mountains.

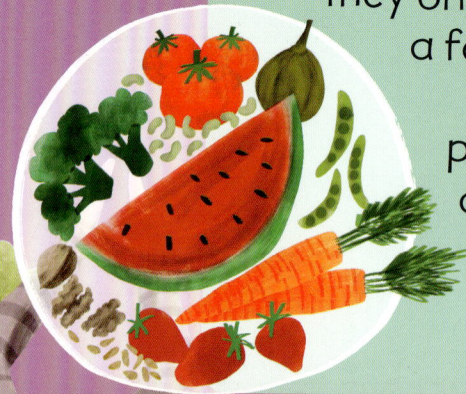

I CAN... BE A HERBIVORE

Bongos, gorillas and colobus monkeys are herbivores — they only eat plants. Plan a family meal that is all made from plants. Eating fruit and vegetables is good for your health and the environment.

Big and busy

The Congo Rainforest is the world's second largest rainforest. The air feels hot and sticky, and near the river, the forest floor turns swampy.

More than 10,000 species of PLANTS live in the Congo Rainforest!

The Congo Rainforest is about 3000 times bigger than the Daintree Rainforest!

I'm a Congo bongo, and I'm a bit shy! I spend my days nibbling on grass and other small plants that grow in sunny spots.

colobus
monkeys

We use branches like trampolines to leap around the canopy.

The fur of old male gorillas turns grey, so they are called **silverbacks**. They protect their family and play with the baby gorillas.

Red river hogs are great swimmers and they love to relax in the cooling mud.

There's safety in numbers! We love to wallow in the water together.

19

Jungles of Borneo

Rainforests are often called jungles. Most jungle animals live in the trees far above the shady forest floor, which is covered in a thick layer of old leaves.

At night, I creep through the branches, listening for bugs and lizards to eat.

SLOW LORIS

Island paradise

Borneo is the largest island in Asia and most of it is covered in dense rainforest. There are animals and plants that live nowhere else on Earth.

Borneo has two seasons: wet and dry. The wet season, or monsoon, lasts from October to March.

Monster flower

The rafflesia grows huge blooms that are up to one metre wide! It makes a foul stink to attract flies to visit it.

Hornbills

Male

Hornbills (label)

I seal my mate up inside a tree hole to keep her safe while she nests. I bring food.

Sealed nest hole

I CAN... LEARN LIKE AN ORANGUTAN

Orangutan mothers teach their babies to recognize the forest trees and learn which ones have tasty fruits and leaves. Learn how to identify and name five types of tree that grow near you.

Nosy neighbours

Proboscis monkeys live in family groups. The males have huge noses and make loud honking sounds.

Orangutan

proboscis monkeys

HONK honk!

We eat leaves.

I use my long arms to climb and swing.

21

The amazing Amazon

It's easy to get lost in the Amazon. It's the world's largest rainforest and home to more animals and plants than any other habitat on land.

At the top

The tallest trees poke up above the rainforest canopy. These are called emergent trees. Parrots and eagles perch in the emergent layer.

TWO-thirds of the Amazon Rainforest is in Brazil.

Harpy eagle

I CAN... HUG A TREE

You can measure a tree in hugs! The older the tree the bigger it will be, so if your chosen tree is old, you may need some help!

My long beak may look strange, but it's great for reaching tasty fruit at the tip of a branch.

22

silky anteater

I find ants' nests in trees. I use my long, curly tail to hang on tight.

giant armadillo

I've got thick skin that protects me like a suit of armour. I use my long claws to dig ants out of their nests.

capybaras

The Amazon River is home to fish, crocodiles and giant rodents called capybaras.

toucan

Danger frogs

Tiny poison dart frogs lurk in the shadows. Their bright colours warn predators that they are coated in a deadly slime that can kill in minutes!

23

The lost forests

The island of Madagascar broke away from Africa more than 100 million years ago. The forests that grow here are at risk of being lost forever.

When I get scared, I leap out of danger – up to one metre into the air!

Precious place

Four out of every five animals that live here are found nowhere else on Earth – and many of them are very strange.

There are fewer than 250 rare **silky sifaka** lemurs left.

Spider tortoise

I bury myself in the forest floor during the dry season.

24

Aye-ayes are lemurs that come out at **night**. They are so shy few people have ever seen one!

Aye-aye

I use my long, skinny finger to dig grubs out of the tree bark.

Fossa

I can run up trees and along branches. I hunt lemurs!

Leaf-tailed gecko

I CAN... USE MY HANDS

Like us, lemurs are primates, so they have hands, each with four fingers and a thumb. Use your hands to make prints in green paint on a large sheet of paper to create a forest scene. Add drawings of your favourite rainforest animals.

Leaf-tailed geckos are masters of **disguise**! They are a type of lizard, but they look like dried up old leaves.

River life

Some of Earth's biggest rivers flow through rainforests. Many animals live in them, and others visit to drink, bathe and cool down.

I CAN... COUNT MY TEETH

Caimans have 72–76 teeth. They are all the same shape — for gripping prey. Use a mirror to count your teeth and look at their different shapes. You have teeth for gripping food, slicing and chewing it.

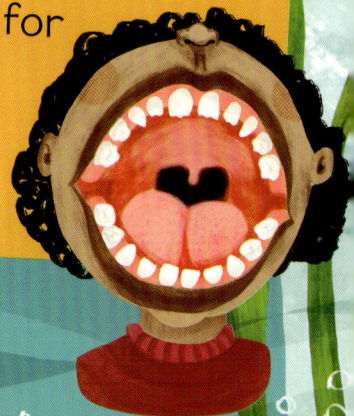

caiman (Costa Rica)

Big and scary

Spectacled caimans are members of the crocodile family that can grow to more than 2 metres long. They lay their eggs on the riverbank and guard their nests.

Green anacondas are **monster-sized** snakes that love swimming.

I use my large paddle-shaped tail to swim through the murky river water.

26

Pink dolphin (Amazon)

Kingfishers perch above the sparkling water and look for fish. They dive in and grab their prey with a long, strong beak.

Malachite kingfisher (Congo)

Pink dolphins

Most dolphins live in the salty sea water, but pink river dolphins live in freshwater instead. Pollution in the rivers is making it hard for them to survive.

Piranhas hunt other fish, often taking big bites out of their fins and tails!

Red-bellied Piranhas (Amazon)

Giant otter (Amazon)

Plants and fungi

Rainforest plants and trees make their own food. They use energy from sunlight to turn water and air into sugars. They return oxygen to the air, help control the weather, and keep the planet cooler.

Epiphytes are plants that grow high on trees so they can reach more sunlight.

Hungry fungi

Fungi don't make their own food — so they aren't plants. They live on plants, animals, or rotting things, and take their food in through root-like threads.

Fungi help break down dead plants and animals into the nutrients that plants need to grow.

Stinkhorn fungus

Mycena toadstool

I munch on toxic leaves. If someone tries to eat me they will be very ill!

Lonomia caterpillar

Lianas are woody plants that cling to trees and hang from their branches.

White-bearded gibbon

Pitcher Plant

Titan arum flower stalks can grow more than 3 metres tall. They stink like rotting fish and eggs. Flies love the smell!

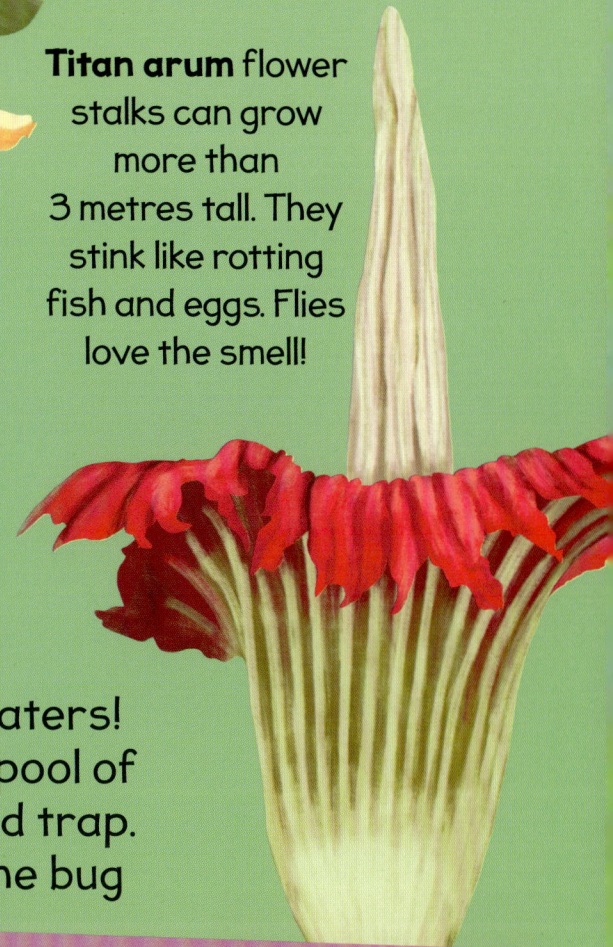

The sugary nectar inside this flower is yummy like honey!

POSSUM

Meat-eaters

Pitcher plants are meat-eaters! Bugs fall in and drown in a pool of water inside the jug-shaped trap. The plant then dissolves the bug and eats it.

Rainforest plants are food for animals. Possums like blossoms!

As I fly between flowers I pollinate them, so they can grow seeds.

I CAN... LEARN HOW PLANTS GROW

The best way to learn about plants is to watch one grow. Plant a bean or tomato seed in a pot of soil or compost. You will need to take care of it and make sure it has water, air and sunlight to make its own food.

Fruits of the forest

Rainforests give us many fruits, nuts and spices. The people who live in rainforests are experts at finding food and living with nature.

Cacao pod

Cacao pods grow on cacao trees. Beans inside the pods are turned into chocolate.

Vanilla pod

Vanilla is a rainforest spice that we use to flavour ice cream, cookies and cakes.

The 'nut' inside an avocado is a seed, which can be used to make red ink.

Avocado

World food

Plants from the jungle are grown all over the world, so everyone can enjoy the fruits of the forest.

Brazil nut tree

Brazil nuts

Many nuts grow on rainforest trees.

Cashew nuts

Cashew tree

Mango tree

Juicy jungle fruits include guavas, durians, rambutans and pineapples.

Mangos

Banana Plant

Bananas

Rainforest people use **WOOD** from **trees** to build their homes and canoes, and burn it to cook their food over a fire.

Many medicines come from rainforest plants.

Tyres from trees

Rubber trees make sticky white goo that can be collected as it oozes from the trunk. This is rubber, and it is used to make tyres and rubber bands.

I CAN... MAKE FRUIT KEBABS

Ask an adult to help you push chunks of different fruits onto kebab sticks, then dip them into melted chocolate for a special rainforest treat! Invite friends or family to share them with you. Can everyone name all the different fruits you have used?

In the treetops

Most rainforest animals live in the canopy (top layer), and have developed clever ways to get around.

Ringtail possums use their strong tails to hang from branches so they can reach fruits and leaves.

Grey-winged longbill

My wingspan is one metre.

A baby fruit bat wraps itself around its mother's belly when she flies.

Flying and leaping

Bats, birds and many bugs fly on wings between trees. Other animals glide, climb or leap instead!

Orange-winged Amazon Parrot

We fly from tree to tree and use our hand-like claws to pick fruit.

I CAN... BALANCE

Running along branches like a monkey takes strength and balance. Build up your skills by standing on one foot for 60 seconds. Then swap feet. Repeat, but now try to balance on one foot with your eyes closed.

Fruit bat

We're just hanging around! We eat fruit, seeds and the pollen inside flowers.

HiSSSSS!

Flying snakes **flatten** their bodies before a leap. They silently **glide** through the air, and take their prey by surprise.

Wallace's flying frog spreads out its webbed toes to glide.

Flying lizards stretch out wide flaps of skin and soar from one branch to another. They can glide 8 metres in one leap!

33

Jungle birds

Birds love rainforests. There are places to perch, nest and hide. There is plenty of food, too — from small bugs and lizards to seeds, nuts and flowers.

Hyacinth macaws are huge, thanks to their long tail feathers.

A macaw can measure one metre from beak to tail tip!

> I've made a lovely bower and decorated it with blue flowers and feathers. I hope she likes it!

Making a home

Birds live in all parts of the forest, from the forest floor to the treetops. Tree holes make safe homes for birds that are caring for eggs and chicks.

Farmyard chickens are close cousins of plump rainforest birds, called junglefowl.

Satin bowerbird

> I look for fallen fruit on the forest floor in the day, but at night I fly up to the canopy to sleep.

southern crowned pigeon

Showing off

Male birds of paradise are glamorous! They dance, sing and show off their fine feathers.

Bird of paradise

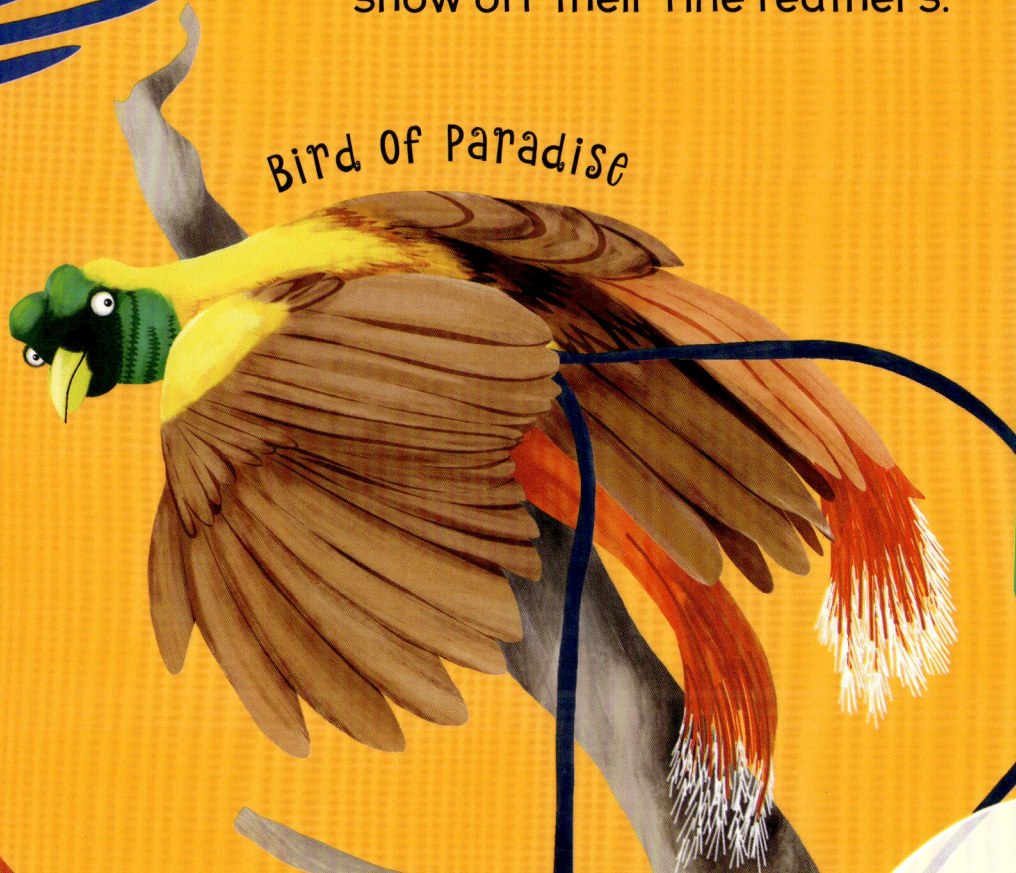

I CAN... NAME THREE BIRDS

Learn about three birds that you can see where you live. Discover what they eat and what their songs sound like. Do they spend all year in your habitat, or do they fly to different places?

chirp!

chirp!

scarlet ibis

I beat my wings in a figure-of-eight shape so I can hover at a flower and sip the nectar.

crimson topaz hummingbird

Bright and beautiful

A stunning scarlet ibis is easy to spot, even in a dense jungle. Groups of ibises perch on trees near rivers and lakes.

Monkeys and apes

Like us, monkeys and apes belong to a group of animals called primates. They are clever, furry animals with hands. Primates live in family groups, and parents teach their babies how to find food.

Chimpanzee

I CAN... COMPARE WEIGHTS

A gorilla weighs up to 200 kilograms. A big howler monkey weighs 10 kilograms. How many of the monkeys would have to sit at one end of a seesaw to balance a gorilla at the other?

Answer: 20

HOWL!!

Howler monkeys are the loudest primates. They can be heard from far away.

When I pull my stick out it will be covered in juicy termites!

Tool-tastic!
Chimpanzees are our closest relatives. They use rocks to smash nuts, and they poke sticks into termite nests to get food.

I use my tail like an extra leg to grab and hold onto branches.

Gibbons **hoot** and **holler** at each other across the treetops. They use their long arms to swing through the branches.

Hoot!

Gibbons

SPIDER MONKEY

Apes don't have tails, unlike most monkeys.

Mountain gorillas

It can get chilly in the African cloud forest. The trees drip, and damp fog hangs in the air, so mountain gorillas need extra-thick fur.

On the prowl

Beware – these predators are silent and deadly! Cats have super senses to see, smell and hear small animals scuttling in the shadows.

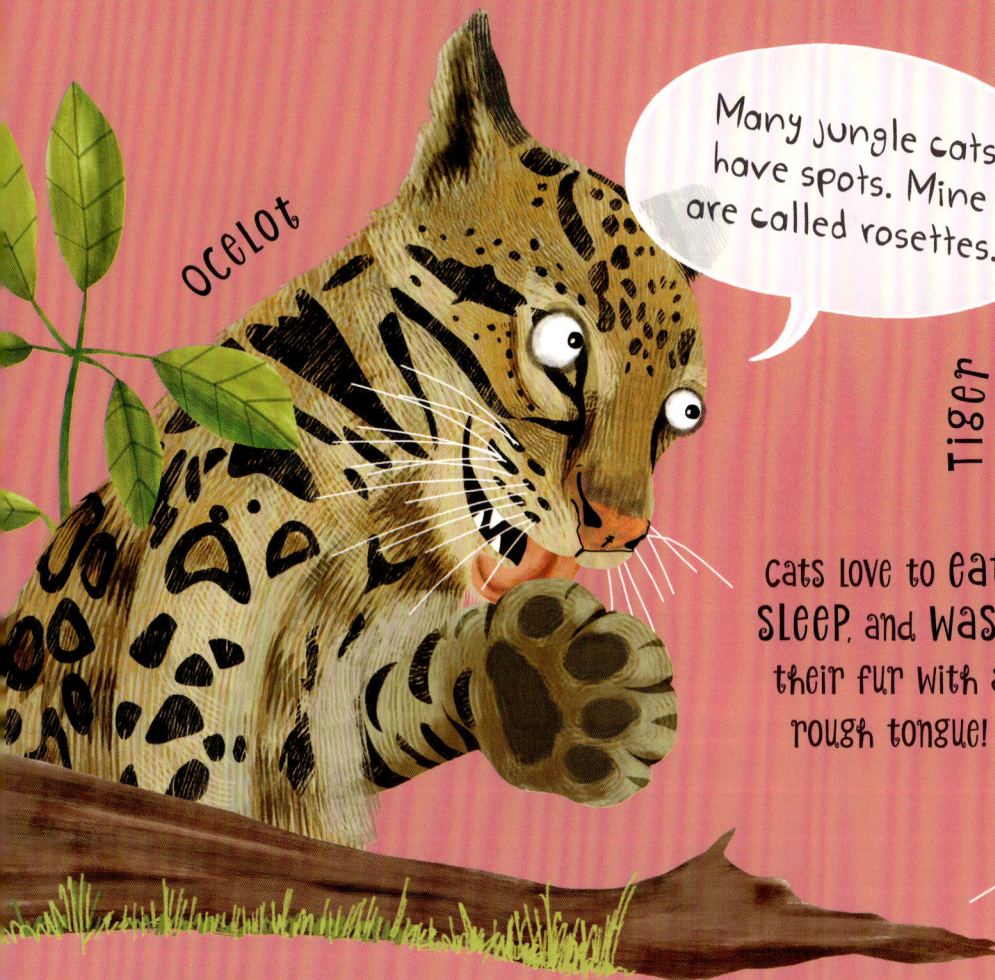

Ocelot

Many jungle cats have spots. Mine are called rosettes.

Tiger

Cats love to eat, sleep, and wash their fur with a rough tongue!

My stripes make it hard for my prey to see me when I'm hiding in shadows or long grass.

Helpful hairs

Whiskers help a cat to feel its way in the dark and work out the size of obstacles or gaps in its path. Whiskers are so sensitive they can even detect changes in the air.

Acrobat cats

Clouded leopards are fast, springy and superb climbers. They spend most of their lives in the canopy, sleeping or chasing monkeys.

Many jungle cats are in danger. People hunt them for their beautiful fur coats.

When I climb down to the forest floor I hunt porcupines, or even grab a fishy treat from the river.

Most cats hate water, but jaguars, like me, love taking a dip in the cooling river.

I CAN... RELAX LIKE A CAT

Cats know how to rest, relax and enjoy quiet time. Stretch your arms and legs, like a cat. Lie down somewhere comfortable. Take ten deep, slow breaths and imagine you are a jungle cat basking in the sun. Enjoy your catnap!

Snakes and lizards

Reptiles are scaly skinned animals that bask in the sun to warm up. Most lay eggs. Snakes and lizards are reptiles, and lots of them live in rainforests.

Gaboon vipers are perfectly camouflaged for life on the brown forest floor. These snakes have long fangs that they use to inject deadly venom.

panther chameleon

I can change colour in a flash. Bright shades show I want to be left alone.

Tongue-tastic!

There are more than 70 types of chameleon on the island of Madagascar. These lizards are often brightly coloured and can catch bugs with a long, sticky tongue!

pygmy chameleon

I'm no bigger than your finger!

coral snake

Snakes and lizards move easily between the **CANOPY** and the **UNDERSTOREY**.

Listen for the sound of a **TOKAY GECKO** calling out for mates.

TO-KAY TO-KAY!

SSSSQUEEEZZZZE!

Constrictor snakes, like me, wrap our coils tightly round our prey and ssssqueeezzzze....

Coral snakes and **milk snakes** look similar, but only coral snakes are venomous. Could you tell the difference if you saw one in a jungle?

MILK SNAKE

I CAN... UNSCRAMBLE THESE WORDS

Here are the names of some types of reptile, but they have been scrambled up. Can you unscramble them?

1. asken
2. adilrz
3. macina

Answers:
1. snake 2. lizard 3. caiman

41

The forest floor

In a rainforest there is a whole world at your feet to explore. Many animals live in this special habitat, including those you can't easily see.

I've buried my egg in a burrow to keep it safe. When it hatches I'll put my baby in the pouch on my tummy.

I CAN... SPOT A REAL FUNGUS

Fungi often have strange names. Which of these are real fungi, and which are made up?

1. Slimy popper
2. Stink hat
3. Pink disco
4. Turkey tail

Answers: 3 and 4 are real

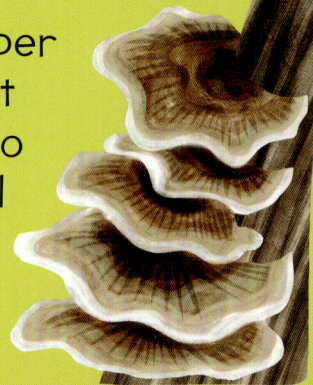

Long-beaked echidnas are unusual mammals because they lay eggs!

Hiding places

It's dark and damp down here, but there are plenty of things to eat and places to hide. Some animals live beneath trees or in underground burrows.

We munch up wood and mix it with our poo to make a lovely mush where fungi grow.

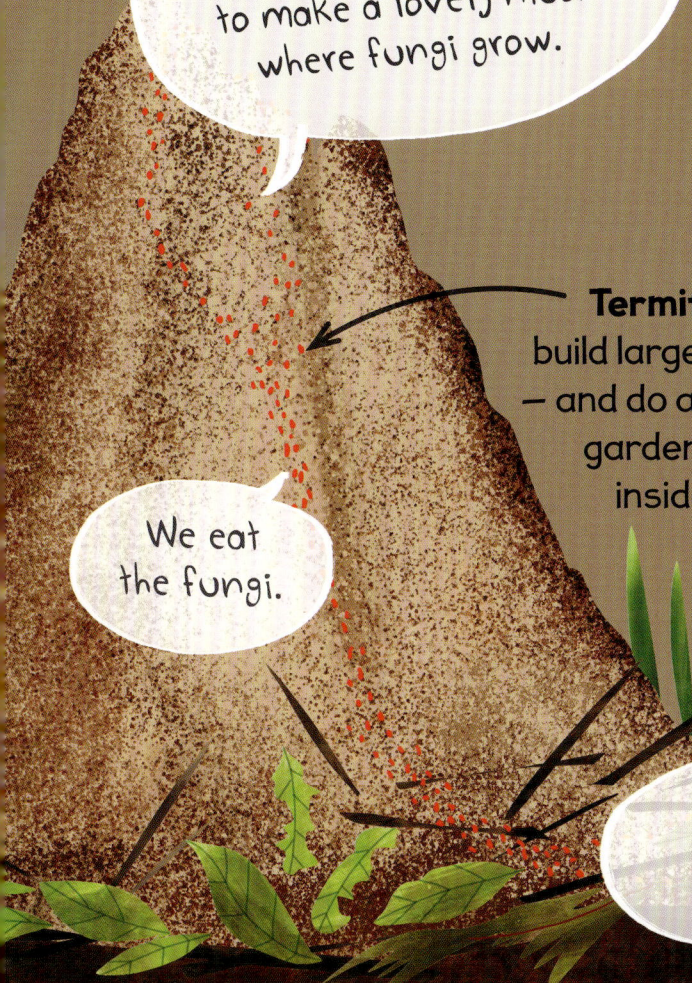

Titan longhorn beetle — world's longest beetle at 14 centimetres!

Termites build large nests – and do amazing gardening inside!

We eat the fungi.

TENREC

I live on the island of Madagascar.

Leaf litter lunch

Small mammals such as tenrecs and shrews look for worms and grubs on the ground.

Sengis are also called **elephant shrews**, because their long, bendy snouts look like trunks.

Follow us onto the next page to find out why we are collecting leaves!

Bugs and spiders

Insects do one of the animal kingdom's most important jobs: they pollinate flowers when they feed on them. This means that the flowers can grow seeds, which will one day grow into new plants.

Fungus farming

Leafcutter ants cut up pieces of leaf, carry them back to their nest, and use them to feed their fungus garden. The ants eat the fungus that grows there and feed it to their babies, too.

Sabre-wing butterflies whizz around above the tall trees, visiting flowers.

Birdwing butterfly

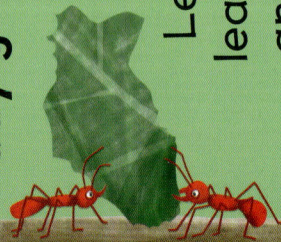

Birdwing butterflies are the world's largest, with a wingspan of 20 centimetres or more.

Praying mantises wait for other bugs to pass by, then attack with a scissor-like grip, holding the victim tight with spiky limbs.

Orb-web spiders spin silk between trees to build sticky webs. Some webs are as large as a person!

Stick insect

I'm perfectly camouflaged on brown twigs in the understorey.

I'm a lacewing caterpillar. When I become a butterfly I'll fly too. But right now I just have to eat, eat, and eat some more!

Bird-eating tarantula

Giant spiders

Tarantulas hunt other bugs, but some are big enough to catch frogs and birds. They kill their victim with a bite and then suck out its insides, like soup!

Orchid bees are brightly coloured in metallic reds, greens and blues. They collect nectar and pollen from orchid flowers.

I CAN... WORK OUT HOW STRONG AN ANT IS

Find out how much you weigh and work out how much you could carry if, like a leafcutter ant, you could carry twenty times your own weight.

WOOLLY Bat

Night time

The sun has set and while some creatures settle down to sleep, others begin to stir. Nocturnal animals usually rest in the day, and are active at night.

Insect-eating **bats** swoop and dive between trees, snapping up flying **bugs**.

Echo hunters

Bats hunt in the dark using a special sense called echolocation. They make click sounds, which echo (bounce off) their prey. The echoes tell them where the bugs are.

I'm going to find something easier to eat!

Leopard

When I get scared I roll into a ball. My hard scales protect me from attack.

Pangolin

Listen for **night monkeys** hooting. Their large eyes help them see in the dark.

A pangolin's tongue is 25 centimetres long! It's sticky, to help it catch ants.

I CAN... INVESTIGATE DAY-LENGTH

Find out what time the sun sets where you live. How long is your daytime, and how long is your night-time? Do these times change through the year, or do they stay the same?

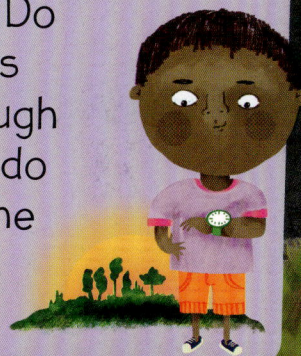

Sunset

In most tropical rainforests day and night each last about 12 hours all year round. The sun sets quickly, turning the forest into an eerie place.

We flash our lights to attract mates to come and visit us in our tree.

Glow worms turn the dark forest into a spectacle of twinkling lights.

Little tarsiers climb through the trees, looking for bugs to eat.

tink tink tink

Little tink frogs call so their mates can find them.

Do you remember?

The information to answer these questions can be found in this book.

How much have you learnt about rainforests?

1 How many seasons do tropical places have?

2 Which ancient creepy-crawly has up to 43 pairs of feet — the velvet worm, or the woolly worm?

3 How many birds visit the Great Bear Rainforest every year?

4 Why do baby tapirs have spots?

5 Does a herbivore eat only meat, or only plants?

6 Which stinky plant grows a flower that is one metre wide?

7 What is the name of the world's largest rainforest?

8 Does the aye-aye have a very big nose, or a very long finger?

9 What colour are the dolphins that live in the Amazon river?

10 Why do chameleons have long, sticky tongues?

Check your answers here!

ANSWERS
1. Two
2. Velvet worm
3. 6 million
4. To help them stay hidden in shadowy places
5. Only plants
6. Rafflesia
7. The Amazon
8. A very long finger
9. Pink
10. To catch their prey

48